It T

Woman

Like Me

I didn't just become, I overcame

By
Kami Jeff-Smith

Table of Contents

Dedication

This book is dedicated to the many people that have been influential in my life in ways that are too many to number. There are so many of my family & friends that I cannot name you all, but there was a token that you dropped along the way. Whether it was a phone call, text, conversation, laugh or even tears we shared that has never gone unnoticed, with you I became.

To my mother Janice, the woman I call my earth Angel. Your strength is not only portrayed from your ability to overcome pain, test, grief, but your ability to still stand in weakness. Short in stature but mighty. You have stood in the gap for me on numerous occasions, staying up at night praying for your family. Your life has been a great example for me to follow on this Christian walk. I will always give thanks in every season of my life as you taught me, "Kami in everything give thanks for such is the will of God concerning you."

To my daughters, Kiana and Jayla, I pray that when you read this book you are reminded that your mother is a warrior and my prayer is that my light shines bright enough to be an example for you. The example that reminds you on your toughest day, that you can and will do anything you put your mind to. Put God first and everything else will follow. Greatness is in your DNA, I love you for life!

To my bonus daughter Skyler, one day I hope it resonates with you on how you welcoming me in your life helped me grow. Your expensive taste was a reminder to me that you don't need anyone's permission to explore and love yourself in many ways. I love you.

To my siblings, April, Gia, Tiffany and Isaac II #teambrownskins lol always remember, everyone brings their own seasonings to the table. This book is just a little extra seasoning to the family recipe, together we make a mighty great meal. We all we got!

To the women who became second mothers to me. My Aunt Bea, Aunt Kam, Aunt Carol & Godmother Mary. You helped raise me, nurture me, correct me and have taught me valuable lessons that I will cherish forever. Thank you for being the strong pillars you are. God bless each of you.

To my spiritual mother and my modern day Naomi, Pastor Zellia Smith of Jehovah Praise and Worship Center, it has been amazing to experience the faith walk with you. I can still hear your words of encouragement every time I thought the weight was getting too heavy. Yould would always remind me and say "Daughter, Don't You Move!"

To my husband Torri, the road isn't and wasn't always easy, but our experience ran me to God. It was only with you that I found my purpose and a closer relationship with God. Thank you for still being you and learning to have a place in your heart that loves me in the process. #824 always ♡

Introduction

I wish I could tell you when I began writing this book I had it all figured out and my broken pieces were mended. I wish I could tell you that life never brings challenges, trials or heartache when you find a relationship with God or that seeking God wholeheartedly, equates to a life held together. What I can tell you is that by the end of reading this book "God is still God!" The Bible reminds us in I Thessalonians 5:18 "In everything give thanks for this is the Will of God concerning you." So remember, no matter the circumstance that you may be faced with at the moment you turn the first page; there is a plan that was predestined before you were created.

I wrote this book for the woman who may be hurting silently. The woman who walks around with a mask pretending to be ok. I wrote this book as a reminder to the abused woman that your strength is within. The person who may be suicidal with no more will to live, you CAN survive. I wrote this book to the Christian woman, who speaks faith but has a lack thereof. The single mother, the jealous woman, the insecure. You see this book is going to speak to the hurt and the pain; but it will also speak to the power you have within, the prayer warrior, the faith walker. The woman who fights for the sanity of her children, who doesn't give up on her marriage, the woman who prays for her enemies. You see the moment you picked up this book, it became the moment you would change your life. I prayed for you, because I was "The Woman Like You."

CHAPTER 1

Reflecting

I can remember the exact day I decided to not give up on myself. It was actually very late one night, I was lying in bed, and instantly, I just sat up and said, "Kami, enough is enough." You know sometimes we make decisions for others, but in this very moment this decision was finally for me. For the prior 2, almost 3 years, I could recall always questioning God and asking, "Why me?" I kept asking month after month, "God, why would you allow me to be in such pain?" I am not talking about the pain of an illness, but a pain that was the heaviness of heart, brokenness, pain of loneliness, pain of confusion, sadness, pain of grief, pain of depression. I was scarred and was enduring great suffering. Our definition of suffering may not be the same, but I assure you that there is an experience that will bring you down to a place where you feel there is no escape. I didn't think I was truly loved by God at the time.

We tend to question God in moments of despair or in the moment when our life is going through a challenging or hurtful season. Have you ever asked yourself how God could love the very thing that He created and allow you to feel so lost, confused, and unloved? I was at a very low period in my life. I was broken, angry, sad, grieving, financially challenged, uncertain about my future, and my mind was all over the place. My mind was a real battlefield at the time, fighting against itself. Day and night, it was a constant fight to find some sense of peace, some sense of understanding where I went wrong. Where did I go wrong in my family life and my marriage? Did I do something wrong or take the wrong path in my spiritual walk? Did I choose the right career? Was I in the right state? Was I even in the right house? Did I marry the right man? I was fighting to understand how I ended up in the places I was in.

I found myself alone, and the money in my bank account was depleting. I found that I was praying for my family, and it seemed that these prayers were not reaching heaven. Tears fell down my face every night; it became a nightly ritual before I finally fell asleep. I sat up in my bed that night and told God, "If you allow this to happen to me, then you must have a greater ending for me." I pondered the saying, "God gives His hardest battles to His strongest soldiers." I guess it was my time to be picked to fight in the battle. I sat there with tears and remembered feeling the urge to write.

My spiritual mother, Pastor Zellia, told me I should write a book about my story. Every time I would have what I'd like to call our phone counseling sessions, she would always say you better write that down for your book. I would laugh it off, and then I found myself agreeing. In the beginning, it didn't register that the pain I was experiencing was to be released into my purpose and a promise. When writing this book, I used memoirs from those exact places. I made up my mind that enough was enough. It was time that my life took an immediate change for the better. I decided to allow all the hurt I was experiencing to be released from me and placed at the feet of God.

A moment of reflection requires you to carefully think. Reflecting will cause one to really identify and consider not the consequences of others but the consequences of one's own actions. A moment of reflection will take you back in time. Sometimes, those moments are scary to relive. That is what occurred during the moments of my writing. I took old journals where I used to write about different events, and I flipped the pages. I was reading years of journaling, and I began to see that there are things in life that we deal with or accept that are truly our own responsibility. There may be events in your life that are beyond your control. I am not speaking on those matters. I can only speak for myself, and as I began to reread my journals and think over my life from a young girl until the adult I had become, I recognized I was in a mess. Mentally and spiritually, I was a mess., I saw myself financially heading into a mess. My marriage was a mess, and my life had been a mess long enough. I had tolerated things and people for far too long. When we tolerate things for too long, we begin to repeat the cycle. I started to reflect on the fact that I was responsible for guiding my life; it was no one else's responsibility but God's and mine. God gave me the power of choice and a conscious mind, and I could choose to be happy or be angry, I could choose to save money, and I could choose to give my life wholeheartedly to God. I could choose to pray for the people who angered me rather than initiating arguments and discord. I could either be mean and intentionally cause harm to others, act out, criticize, or be a woman whose actions are led by love. I reflected that every action and reaction to things was all owned by me.

I made a conscious effort to no longer focus on why people do what they do but rather on what my actions would be. I took total control of myself and decided that I would make every effort to always be led with love. I became cautious of what words I allowed to come out of my mouth. I started acknowledging that I had a huge part in my life that didn't always look as nice as it seemed. I started by forgiving myself and asking God to forgive me for anything that was displeasing in His sight. I am glad that God sent his son Jesus, who shed His blood, so that we may have a right to His open arms of forgiveness. No matter the act, no matter the time it takes you, God welcomes us with open arms. God takes the most unattractive pieces of us and creates beauty from ashes.

Those who hurt me, I decided to forgive them even without them asking. That was tough for me because for quite some time in my adult years of experiencing hurt, for some reason, I felt like some people (it wasn't many) owed me an apology. If you had hurt me in some capacity, I thought I deserved an apology, and I waited for it. I was holding the hate and anger, and all along, I had the power to stop the bleeding on the self-inflicted wound. I looked back over my life and freed myself from my past. The freeing of my past was not an immediate experience; this was not a quick fix or a snap of your finger and clicking your heels 3 times, and a new me appeared. No, this took time. This only came from weeks, months, and over a year of constant prayer, reading the Bible, speaking over my life, and fasting. There were moments when I had to totally disconnect from family and friends during this time, and I was in a place that required me to experience God on a higher spiritual level. It was mandatory for me to walk with power. I shed the old skin, and I never looked back.

Think about this, when you pause and reflect on your life, are the things you put out on this earth truly how God wants to see you? I can admit that I have said things I shouldn't, wished bad on others and waited for them to suffer, intentionally walked a life unpleasant to God, provoked someone to anger, invaded someone's privacy, and a number of things I am not proud of. We all have sinned and come short of the glory of God; in fact, we were born into this world as sinners. There is no sin that is greater than the next. I, too, was a sinner and needed to be cleansed, corrected, humbled, and forgiven. The good thing about our heavenly Father is that He will forget those things, forgive us, and not throw them back on our faces as some people do. He said in *Hebrews 8:12, "And their sins and their iniquities will I remember no more."* You have to remember this, leave the past in the past, leave your sin in the past.

It took me almost 48 years for my eyes to open and finally get to the peak of the mountain. My peak of the mountain was my desire for a life of peace and happiness, days where I woke up and felt the presence of God, and the air I breathed became a fresh air of peace and sanity and where

God's goodness seemed to run after me. If you ever had to climb a mountain, then you know that the closer you get to the top, the harder the climb begins to feel. The higher the climb, the more you get the feeling of altitude sickness, and you begin to feel like your oxygen is getting cut off. Little do you know that if you keep going through these difficult times, you will be almost at the destination. At one point in my life, I felt like my life was coming together, and I was finally experiencing a place of happiness. It was around the year 2015 that I was promoted to a management role for a Fortune 500 company. I had just sold my home, my money was good, my kids were healthy, I was living in peace, spent weekends riding bikes on the beach, went to the finest restaurants, was smiling, traveling, and finally had opened my heart to dating, loving my life and the people in it. I was almost to that peak of the mountain, but low and behold, fast forward, and a few years later, I found I was right back where I started. I started feeling sadness, and my life was incomplete. I was like, God, is this a joke?

You can think you are on the right path in your life, skipping along to a new mindset, changed behavior, and a new life full of contentment and happiness. Then, before you know it, you take the wrong turn, and that turn brings you to a complete stop. I made a few wrong turns and had moments where it seemed I was at a dead end. Sometimes, it only takes one bad turn. I took a turn down the lane of overspending and depleting savings, thinking because I had money in the bank, I didn't need to work when, in actuality, if I had worked, I would have been increasing my savings and building a strong financial future. I took the wrong turn of dating when I should have been healing and learning the true meaning of being whole without a man and learning to love me. I took the wrong turn of not being faithful to God as I was worshiping God on Sunday but still sinning and pleasing my flesh rather than pleasing Him. I took turns, which caused me detours and delays. Do you know that you can cause things to be delayed in your life? Your delay comes from the choices you make, the people you attach to, the character you possess, and most importantly, the Christian walk you choose. Have you ever heard someone say you are causing a delay to your blessing just by the people you are with or the company you keep? Maybe you are delaying your blessing because you won't stop sinning. I delayed my own blessings because of how I chose to respond to my life.

It just hit me, and I woke up and realized the person I have been, "THAT WOMAN," I no longer wanted to be her. I no longer wanted to feel sorry for myself. I no longer wanted to walk around with a heavy heart. I no longer wanted to lay in bed at night and struggle to sleep. I no longer wanted to blame anyone for the way I was feeling. I no longer wanted to feel what I was feeling. Some people call it the a-ha moment or the light switch that finally turns on; some may say you received a revelation. I felt like I had been given this one last chance to see what my life could really be and I held on to it in that very moment. I was literally holding so tight to God as Jacob did when he wrestled with the Angel. I held on and said God, I won't let go until you bless me. I won't let go until I see a difference in me and my circumstances.

You cannot imagine the lack of faith I had. There were years of tears; I mean, I was at the point of filling up a river; I had cried so much. I was stuck in a rut of rejection. I stopped and said, "God, I give my heart to you." I lay this pain at your feet, Jesus, the man that heals the brokenhearted, the man who renews your mind, the man who, before I was formed in my mother's womb, knew me. God, the great I AM, the redeemer, the Author, and the Finisher, The Beginning and the End, the First and the Last, the Almighty God, our Father. At that moment, I said, "God, make me into the woman you created me to be!!"

You are here right now reading this very first Chapter because "IT'S GOING TO TAKE A WOMAN LIKE YOU." Yes, you! A powerful young lady, a woman of wisdom, mother, sister, daughter, aunt, pastor, prophetess, teacher, grandmother, entrepreneur- yes, you! IT TOOK A

WOMAN LIKE ME to become fearless, powerful, and ready for the battle. I walked with pure faith, and after reflecting on my circumstances, I got up from that place. Tell yourself that you are a woman of God walking into the most beautiful time of your life. I know you may not see it, looking at where you are at this second. I encourage you to stop and take a moment to reflect on your life and then begin to believe that where you are is just the bridge to the next level of you. You don't have to spend another day of your life the same way. Let God heal you from your past. Let God heal you from every broken piece, every person, every word, every thought, everything that has caused you any harm or hindrance in you moving into this new season. Get on the path and stay on it. Even when it feels like it is too difficult to reach the peak of your mountain, keep climbing.

CHAPTER 2

Break The Curse

There are moments in our lives when we finally grab hold of our purpose, the very reason we were created. My Apostle Dennis, in his Sunday sermons, has often mentioned that there are numerous people at the graveyard who have never tapped into their purpose. They let life pass them by, and the one thing that they were created to accomplish, that was embedded in them to execute, never came to fruition. You can be on the road to your purpose and can easily make a detour because the road gets rough. The bumps slow down your pace, and you exit right before you reach your final destination. I wrote this book during a period in my life when healing began. I started to see that I smiled more, and I recognized that my heart was no longer weary with heaviness; I was no longer alone. I learned what the meaning of loving myself meant. God became my firm foundation. The healing experience brought the realization that my pain had a purpose. We are accustomed to fuelling pain for pity, but I fueled my pain to propel my passion and purpose.

The Bible tells us that before we were formed in our Mother's womb, God knew us. This means with every second of our life, God already knew exactly the very first breath we would take, the moment we were conceived, our very first fall, the relationships we would have, the first car we would drive, our first heartbreak, the family we would be born into and every pain and blessing that would be time stamped to the very millisecond. I was born at Holy Cross Hospital in 1976 in the State of Florida. Maybe being born in the Holy Cross was a sign that God knew He would use me from birth. I was the middle child of 5 children, 3 sisters, April, Gia, and Tiffany, and one brother, Isaac II, the youngest. Many people always recognized my sister Gia and me as twins because we were very close in height, though we were 10 months apart. She is the oldest, and I was born a bit premature, and the reason for the 10-month difference. I had a loving mother, Janice, and a hard-working father, Isaac. I was always surrounded by love and the love of my family. We had a very strong bond; we traveled, and we grew up knowing the streets and the church (more church than street). That is what happens when your mother makes it her business to raise you in the church, but your father makes certain you are not blinded to the ways of the street.

17

I used to think that, as a child, I was different. I won't say I was the black sheep, but in my mind, I was just different. My siblings say I was my mother's favorite; I think that was because I favored her. I used to think I was both parents' favorite (I won't argue that in this book, lol.) We had a good life, I would like to think. We had many laughs and occasional tears, but we never went without. I always seemed to be the child who helped calm situations and brought reason to the family.

God knew my name before I was conceived. He had hand-picked me to do His work. I would not understand this until I became an adult. My purpose was to reach other women to find their greatest selves through some of their hardest periods in life. My ministry was to push you into your purpose even during the exact moment you feel like you are at your lowest possible point. I was there, and I must warn you that when you finally identify that there is something great that lies within you, you then realize you have to "BREAK THE CURSES" over your life that hold you back from your greatest self.

As an adolescent, you may have been taught in school that in order to solve a problem, you must first define the root cause of the problem. Life can present itself as a bit of a challenging problem that takes years to address or resolve.

Identifying the root cause of a problem is the initial step towards its resolution. I can sit here and make what I need to say sound really pretty or educated, but the ugly truth is we all need help in some area of our lives. We all have a curse that needs to be broken. We all have a place where we have been damaged. To this day, I can still cry as I write the words "need help."

If you are like me, I never wanted to portray a sign of weakness to anyone or make anyone think I needed anything, let alone help. Acknowledging you need help is an excruciating phrase to form your mouth to say. Admitting you need help, especially when everyone looks at you as a person with the capability of being the go-to, the problem solver, or the pillar, can be quite difficult to admit. If you never admit you have a flaw, as we all are flawed, and if you never admit that you can improve or change that one thing or things that show the ugly side of you, then you can never grow. Growth requires change, and change will be uncomfortable, but it will be worth it.

The problem or curse we are looking to break may be considered a generational curse. Curses that have been connected to you from your parents or grandparents. This is the mere fact that you were genetically connected to your problem. Some people blame their curse by using the popular excuse, "This is just who I am." Let's face it, we all have some issues. We all have, at some point in time, been confused about what really makes us who we are or why we react the way we do. Why do we become jealous? Why do we feel depressed? Why are we angry? Why are we insecure? Why do we feel unloved or sad for some reason? Why do we speak negatively about ourselves? Why do we compare ourselves to other women? Why do we hold a heart of unforgiveness? Why do we, as women, look for validation from everyone except validation from within? Why have we been ok with sleeping with someone else's husband? Why are we just nasty for no reason? Why do we dislike other women because of their success? Why do we hate the next woman without knowing her real story? Why do we lie, cheat, and hate the people God sent to love us and cling to the people who are just bad for our mental, spiritual, and physical health?

This is the beginning of the story, where you have to be real with yourself and say, "God, I need help.." It's important to understand you can't start a healing process until you're woman enough, or man enough, to own your own mistakes and acknowledge the areas you need to grow in. Admit that you have issues in which you seem to remain stagnant, the place where you find yourself repeating with no progress.

These are the things you know you should change but have made a choice not to address.

As I was writing this book, my husband Torri asked me a question, and it stuck with me from the moment he said it. "Kami, do you want to tease them or HELP them?" He always had a way with words that made me think. I didn't always like to hear him out, especially when he was right. I couldn't always receive his advice, especially during times when I was upset or displeased with him. How many times have you ever blocked out what someone was saying that was beneficial to you just because of who the messenger was? Don't miss the message because of who God sent to be the messenger. Not every message will come to you as a person dressed in a suit with a Minister's collar or a fancy title. At the end of their Name. One lesson I had the pleasure of hearing was from a woman with no degree; she once said, "Don't make decisions from your emotions, but ask yourself what your heart is saying to you." We learn some of the most valuable lessons from the people we least expect. Don't discount the woman on the corner or the man with a bottle in his hand because they can teach you a thing or two about life. On this specific occasion, I could hear my spouse loudly and clearly only because I was in a mature posture to receive it.

I said to myself before writing this book that I can't give the reader everything, and there are some parts where I first held back. Then I remembered my divine purpose was to help the next woman and how I could accomplish that by not releasing my experience in its entirety. This is the part of my story where I share one of the reasons why I needed help. I had been carrying a curse that needed breaking. I can remember I needed help in a major way. If I can keep it real with you, I must tell you just how much I needed the help. I carried a pain that I camouflaged really well, a pain that started as a young adult and progressively got worse with time. It was a pain of mental and emotional hurt. It caused me to question my self-worth.

Fast forward to the year 2006, to the moment in my life, I realized I was strong enough to stay but too weak to leave. Read that again. I was in love with a man, and we had been dating for almost 7 years; we never married, but we had what seemed in the beginning to be a good life. This man never hit me or abused me physically, but I was definitely hurt in my mind. If you have ever experienced mental or emotional abuse, it leaves a scar that takes time and pure healing from God. Many women stay in relationships too long and cause damage to themselves emotionally and sometimes physically. I had a close friend who was physically abused, and I never understood why she just couldn't leave. I saw how she would be beaten but then be showered with gifts and given quite the amount of cash, and that seemed to just make her feel better, I assumed. I even remembered calling the cops once after witnessing a brutal fight, and she turned around and was very angry with me. I didn't understand it, yet years later, I realized I was no better than her as I stayed in a place where I knew I wasn't mentally and emotionally healthy.

Like many women and men, I stayed in an on-and-off-again relationship with promises of change, only to be met by the cycle repeating itself because there was never any real healing. I stayed too long and the longer I stayed the more I cried silently alone, and smiled in public. I was emotionally damaged, so damaged I started asking myself if something was wrong with me.

I remember after an argument, I would wait to cry in the shower. I did this so my daughter Kiana couldn't see my tears. I was really beginning to worry about what my daughter would think; I was more worried for Kiana since she was the oldest, and Jayla was 9 years younger, so she didn't understand. It seemed like the smallest thing would upset him. I couldn't hide my tears much longer because my daughter was getting older and starting to feel the pain. Don't get me wrong, he was providing for our family financially, but there was no amount of money that could stop the sadness I was feeling. Do you know if you are not careful, you can cause mental harm to your own children by the relationships and people you connect to? I started believing I would always be in this place of agony. I started believing I was going crazy. That's what he would say to me, "Kami, something is wrong with you." He would have terrible mood swings, happy one minute and upset the next, a pure Dr. Jekyll & Mr Hyde experience. I was wondering, because of his angry outbursts, if he was cheating and I did something to cause it. If I asked him a question like, "Do you love me?" he would lead me to believe I was crazy. You know, if someone tells you these things long enough, you begin to believe them. I eventually learned that he was deflecting his flaws upon me.

I stayed because the houses were big, the money was good, and it appeared I was living the life. Like a lot of relationships, every day was not all bad; there were trips, gifts, and times I really felt loved and put up on a pedestal. Before I knew it, I began to feel like I was walking on eggshells daily. I was cautious about what to say because I didn't want to trigger an argument and would think of everything I could do to keep him from getting upset. I even had my daughter Kiana be careful what she would say and if he had a chore for her just to complete it with no complaint. There are people who will inflict you with their mental pain and their childhood trauma and really walk around like they have no issues. To the outside world, they have such a great role, but in their home, they are the true opposite. This type of person can be so damaged that they are blind to their own flaws. Sadly, I was living a life that was damaging, and I didn't know how to leave. I remember crying one day, and I said to him, "I want you to just let me go."

Leaving became the hardest thing for me to do. It was years later that I finally did. I purchased my own home, and it was done in faith. I told God, "If you help me, God, I will leave." God paved the way for me to have a new construction property, and I barely put a dime down out of my own pocket. That was faith the size of a mustard seed coming to life. I remember walking into the model home of the subdivision, where the young lady began to show me different floor plans and models. In conversation, she began to tell me how she had recently relocated and found this job working for the builder. She discussed how she moved to the state because she needed a new start from a relationship. She moved, and all she had were her clothes and money for gas. We walked into one of the houses, and she looked at me and said, this will be your home. She was absolutely correct. That was the very house I closed on! I never saw her again throughout the entire time I was closing on the property. I am certain God had placed her on my path for one reason. This was over 15 years ago, and I have often told that story to women who are going through a tough relationship and are not sure if they have the will to exit. So today, I tell you, never give a man or anyone that level of power over you. Take that power, pull yourself together, and pack up. God will move you. He will move your feet when you are not sure how to walk away. He will also break you in the process, but He will rebuild you and make way for you.

Love can hold you in places you do not belong. You're hurting, but you still believe it's love. My father once told me, "Kami love doesn't hurt." I am not telling you that a person cannot get better because, with God, all things are possible. I have seen God take a man and clean him all the way up. He did it for my own father. God can work miracles in men to become great husbands, great fathers, great Leaders in Ministry, great influencers in the community, etc. It was just that season, and I had no other choice but to leave. God began to break the curse off my life as I walked out the door.

My negative experiences in life were a result of my lack of trust in myself and others and my lack of self-worth. This same hurt and pain that I carried I took with me to my next relationship. That curse even infiltrated into my marriage. Prior to marrying Torri, I believed I was living my best single life. I was telling myself that I was healed and over my past. But I wasn't. I took trips, went on dates, and spent money spoiling myself; I was really feeling good about myself. I had enough money to finance my lifestyle and looked really good doing it. Sadly, I was still walking around emotionally unhealed, trying to fill voids. I didn't take the time to really seek spiritual counseling or regular counseling because I always seemed to think when you walk away from something or someone, your new beginning is supposed to bring you to a complete stop and erase your past. It's not true. If you're at this place and you are telling yourself this, it is a lie. Healing is not an overnight or weekend process.

You must heal; you must break the curse so that in the next relationship you encounter, you are free to love wholeheartedly. In 2018, I was still bleeding from my past when I married Torri. If you want to know the truth, Torri and I both had blood on our hands. I acted out of the hurt I had received from someone else; most people do the same. Anything Torri did that seemed questionable I immediately felt was a lie. I started to replay events that had happened years prior in a previous relationship, and immediately, my mind called him a liar without proof. I would think every moment away from him, he must be cheating. This happens to people who have experienced similar hurt, and they question everything because that is what they know. There is truth behind the saying "hurt people hurt people." I had a horrible time trusting because I was holding on to past trauma. Don't get me wrong, there are people who lie, cheat, and are narcissistic, and your intuition is spot on. There are cases where you doubt the relationship or person because of a previous experience. I learned a tough lesson through all of this. Your past belongs to you, and it should never be anyone's responsibility to carry the weight of your past.

God, becoming first in my life, stopped the bleeding. The blood of God washed me. I had no other place or person to run to who could help me besides the Man who created me. I had to begin to ask God to help me release the negative thoughts in my head and break me free from the chain that was holding me. I prayed and spoke that I was no longer bound by a curse. I asked God to release me from any soul tie to anyone from my past. You do know that soul ties are real, so be careful of all the people you allow access to you. I mean the people you are intimate with because you are opening yourself up to the spirits of not just that person but their past partners or their sexual partners that they are still involved with while claiming to be faithful to you. It is real. That is the reason the Bible teaches us that our bodies are a Temple of the Holy Ghost; your body is sacred. It should not have people going in and out like the 24-hour corner store. Save it for the person that God sends you.

I was on my path to healing and got counseling from my church leaders and even took the time to speak to a psychiatrist. Even a conversation with my mother would get me through a hard time. Ultimately, my true help came from God. I made it my business to stay in prayer, read the Bible, speak positive affirmations, fast, and spend quality time with God. Today, I make it a habit of saying I am in a ready state to give all of myself to the man God created just for me. You know the saying, "I give you all of me!" That has to be first to God, and then you will recognize real love. I want to always be in the position and stand in the posture to be able to feel the freedom of knowing how to love without being triggered by my past. That's a different kind of love. That is real Christian love, love without limits, love without condition, the Agape love. First, learn to love yourself. You have to be so confident in the love you have for yourself that when you meet a special someone, you don't look for them to complete you. Loving yourself requires understanding God's love for you.

Stop blaming everyone else for where you are, and look first at yourself. One of the hardest things for you to admit is that you held on to a pain that was just familiar. You held on, and you continued day after day, month after month, year after year, carrying the heavyweight. Sit and think for just a moment; maybe you did this because it was something you continued to bandage. Maybe you really never knew where to start or how to find the help you needed. Maybe, you had temporary satisfaction that caused you to keep overlooking and pushing this one thing to the backburner of your monthly to-do list.

Can I just tell you, that what you are going through in your life right now is a survival guide for someone coming behind you. There is another woman that will experience the same exact pain you are feeling today and you will have to reach back to tell her she can make it through. There will come a time that you will be speaking to a total stranger, as I experienced, and the revelation will kick in after you hear her story and understand your conversation was not by accident. I found myself on numerous occasions talking to women, and they would naturally begin to open up to me about their life and their pain. After speaking to them, I started understanding that God was in that moment, building up their faith based on my real-life experiences of how I made it to the point in my life. They would say, "You seem so strong," but they had no idea the nights I had cried or the days I was weak. They didn't know the curse that I carried for so many years. They only saw where God had taken me.

The Bible says we are overcome through our testimony. It will be your testimony that just might save the next woman. It took me too many years to wake up and realize, "Kami, you are walking around like the woman with the issue of blood in the Bible." In *Luke 8:43-48,* the Woman walked around for 12 long years with an issue of blood, and it only took one touch from God for her to be made whole. Her faith is what healed her. So I ask you, "Do you want to walk around for years the same way, or do you want to be made whole and break the curse?

There are times we look to protect our self-image. We desire to have a positive outlook on others, so we pretend our life is a pretty painting on a clean wall. We can wear the finest clothes and paint our faces with makeup, presenting ourselves to the world as a beauty queen, but have you ever asked yourself, "What am I feeding my soul?" It took me a minute to understand that it's okay to ask for help, and it's okay to say you're not okay. It's ok to seek spiritual counseling. It's ok to say no and to have a moment alone. It's ok to acknowledge the pain and remove yourself from anything that is causing you harm or causing you to walk away from God. Make God first! If you don't get anything else from this Chapter, at least grab hold of the importance of allowing God to take the wheel. The issues that you have had all this time can and will be broken off your life. Take God at His word and bring your issues, your brokenness, and your past hurt to Him. Aren't you tired of crying over the same thing? Aren't you tired of being bitter? Aren't you tired of just being broken? Aren't you tired of hurting and having that nasty attitude? Aren't you tired of being tired? Allow God to fight every battle and allow Him to lead you into a life worth living, a life of victory.

A curse over your life can be broken by the realization that you want to be freed, that you want to be healed and delivered. God loves you, and He wants your whole heart; God wants you to know you are loved, and God wants you to know that the burden you are carrying, He says, "Cast your cares on me because I care for you." Break free from the chains that have held you captive, look in the mirror, and tell yourself, "I am free because who the Son sets free is free indeed." The enemy wants to hold you in a place so you cannot grab hold of peace, a life filled with happiness, joy and love. You must first acknowledge what has been holding you captive and then say it today, "You have no power over me any longer." I am free, and my power comes from God. The place that you are going to can only take A WOMAN LIKE YOU to endure. I know because it TOOK A

WOMAN LIKE ME to fight the enemy one-on-one, and God broke the chains that held me captive for so many years. I am free to open my heart to love. Always remember that we don't just learn from hurt; we love from the places of hurt.

CHAPTER 3

Take The Mask Off

I remember one of my sisters once said to me, "Your strength was your weakness," and I can also recall her words in another setting, "Kami, Miss Perfect Patty." I didn't really realize it back then, but in my own world, I wanted to be seen as close to perfect, having my life together, and as good in the eyes of others. I always wanted to appear strong and never bothered, but that wasn't the case. I had created a persona as if I was never disturbed.

I can remember when Torri and I began dating, we would chat on Facebook, and he sent me a meme that said: "Take off the mask when you're talking to me." I was surprised he sent it, but the reality is that we all do it. We pretend to showcase strength on the outer layer, but the internal man is weak, damaged, bruised, broken, abused, tired, and weary. At a young age, I found myself wanting and having this strong desire to just be liked. I remember always comparing myself to my siblings, as I was the daughter with the darkest complexion of all the girls. I thanked God when my brother was born, we became "Teambrownskins." I can laugh about it now, especially as my youngest sister seems to make herself a part of our group, loving and embracing this beautiful dark-melanated skin. Even still, it brought out my insecurities as I became an adult. I figured if I was going to be different, at least I would be liked, if nothing else. I found myself being a people pleaser to win over friendships. I did have a sweet spirit about myself, but I always felt like I was putting in extra effort to accomplish friendships. I was very insecure about myself as a young adult because I looked different and took those deep-rooted feelings with me for years. I questioned if I was good enough, pretty enough, and if I stood above others. No matter who, man, woman, boy, or girl, said I was beautiful, I just always seemed to ask myself, was I really? I would go into a relationship with the desire for validation. I had been awaiting true validation from others. But the problem was I never truthfully validated myself.

I can remember as a little girl, I had to have everything just right. My grades had to be perfect, and I had to get straight A's. I wanted my skin perfect; I would wash my face constantly out of fear of having marks or pimples. I remember walking past the mirror in our living room and checking my skin frequently to make sure there were no pimples. My clothes and shoes had to be lined up perfectly, and the bedroom was cleaned to perfection. When things would fall out of place, I would literally cry. I remember my parents moving my siblings into a different room because they were not as clean as me. I ended up sharing my room with my youngest brother [name], and I do not think it is by coincidence that he is very organized today. While I can laugh at the story now, the reality was that when anything seemed out of place or out of my control, I lost it. I would have a mental meltdown, and it began to cause me to act unlike myself. I would do whatever was necessary to put what was out of place into the place I desired. That might have come with me getting upset and verbalizing it or getting really quiet until I could come up with a quick fix to satisfy myself. Even as an adult, I will constantly clean. My kids and stepkids can tell you this firsthand. I knew it drove them crazy. They always knew if I was upset or thinking because I would go into cleaning mode.

It didn't stop with me wanting to be a perfect image or have my life and the things around me in a perfect place; I also started self-sabotaging with negative thoughts and events that never occurred. The Bible says in *James 1:8, "A double-minded man is unstable in all his ways."* My actions definitely included being double-minded. These types of actions are not of God, and it takes a strong individual to recognize that and a stronger individual to dismiss the negativity. Go ahead and admit, like me, that sometimes your mind is a battlefield. You can think yourself into a false narrative and shift a good day into a bad day by just your act of what you begin to think. Sometimes, we tell ourselves the opposite of what God speaks about us. God says that you are made in His image, a royal priesthood, a chosen generation, far greater than rubies, and everything God made is GOOD. You have to speak to the thoughts and redirect everything negative you say about yourself.

I had perfected the art of masking because it was an embarrassment for me to look weak. I was uncomfortable with the perception of looking like I didn't have it all together, and the truth was, I was a mess on the inside. I am sharing this with the woman who has walked around with a mask, raincoat, rain gear, and rain boots and is expecting it to rain. The woman who is expecting rain in the midst of a sunny day. You are mentally preparing for storms that are not there. You could be in a conversation with me and tell me something or an event or just talk about what happened in your day, and if your tone sounded awkward or maybe you were pausing too many times or stumbling over words, I would immediately go into a negative thought. I would immediately think you were a liar or not being completely honest. I was making your story a lie when, in actuality, you could really be truthful. That was me creating a storm in my mind. We create storms in our lives when we should be living and loving in the moment and embracing the good of the day. Instead of picturing the day ahead with success, we can tend to bring destruction. I smiled during the day and was masking what my thoughts really were.

The truth is we mask our way through life. We have no perfect limb in our bodies. Instead of attending to the broken pieces of ourselves (red flags), we live with the limp, and years later, we are more damaged than ever. I finally had to stop masking my life and begin to be ok with the fact that I was not perfect and didn't have to please anyone but God. I was ok with being different. I was made different by God for a special reason. God did not need two of me; He only needed one, and I was enough. Every day was not meant to be a perfect day. Things will get out of place; some days may be chaotic, but you don't have to fight to fix everything. Sometimes, God allows things to fall out of place so He can put it all back together. I began to look at my life and realize I was missing so many great moments because I was looking for what could go wrong rather than just living in the moment and letting things happen on their own. I started to see the beautiful life God created for me, and no matter what happened in the day, I remembered a saying my father told me: "Let it roll off your back, like water on a duck, IT DON'T STICK!"

The negative thoughts that you are having are also canceled off your life; you are no longer head sick. You are free to love yourself; the woman you are is enough, and you are healed. Do you know that life and death are in the power of the tongue? Speak the good things about yourself; speak life every morning you wake up. I don't think we know how powerful our words are. You can actually speak blessings or curses because God said we are speaking beings. Speak from the God-given power within and allow every great thing about you to manifest. People are either going to love you or hate you. You don't have to pretend to be someone you are not. Let people love you where you are, and if they are not for you, let God remove them. Free yourself from the mask. The mask is no longer; God says who the son sets free is free indeed. You are free! Show the world the beautiful being that God created. You can TAKE THE MASK OFF and walk around free.

CHAPTER 4

Be Still

One of my favorite scriptures in the Bible is *Psalm 46:10, "Be still, and know that I am God: I will be exalted among the heathen, I will be exalted in the earth."* There comes a point in your life where you will have to experience being in a place of stillness. It is in the struggle of stillness that we meet God, and we meet ourselves. I remember, in my younger adult years, always wanting to be around others or feeling like I had to have a man to fill me or complete me. I never wanted to experience the noise of loneliness.

In 2021, God put me in a place of being alone, and there was nothing I could do to prevent it. There was no prayer at the time, and I could not pray to Him to change my situation. Have you ever experienced deafening silence? Let me just tell you that being still, sitting still, and doing nothing can be quite challenging for some. It was the hardest challenge I have faced to date. I was faced with what I like to call my hardest test as a Christian woman. I was alone;

yes, I was a wife, a mother, a sister, an Aunt, a friend, a Real Estate Entrepreneur, a Supervisor, a prayer warrior, a Praise Team member, a Pastoral board member, and I was alone.

I can tell you firsthand that alone time will force you to hear a noise you can't silence. It was just a few years before I started writing I found myself alone. I remember the day like it was yesterday. I was sitting in the living room, and not even an hour after we had eaten breakfast and watched a movie, I watched silently as my spouse, Torri, walked out the front door. I sat and watched him pack his bags and carry them out the door, and I never stopped him. I cried no tears that day, no fighting, no argument, but it was a day I will never forget. This day was embedded in my memory. The keen focus here in this Chapter of BEING STILL is not merely the reason he was no longer in the place he promised and vowed he would be, to love me and honor me, in sickness and in health until death, but the fact of what was my stance and position when he walked out.

God forced me into a place where it was now just Him and I, now.! It was the greatest test I had ever faced. If the door had never closed that day and I saw the back of my husband facing me, I would have never had the experience of being alone. I had never in my life really ever been in this place. I was never put in this predicament because the majority of my other relationships were on my terms. Even when the road got really bad in my previous relationship, I mentioned it was me who left, not the other way around.

I felt completely rejected, disrespected, angry, and raged, but at the same time, I was numb. You will understand later in the book just why I was so numb at that moment. I didn't think this would ever happen to me because, yes, I felt I was a keeper, a real good woman. I felt like it didn't get much better than me, and I deserved a good man and a good marriage. I thought if I kept a clean home, worked, kept myself up, cooked a good meal, packed his lunch, and loved him in more ways than one when he asked, my answer was yes 97% of the time, I would never reject him. I thought if I washed his clothes, rubbed his head and massaged his back, became a mother to his kids, went to church and prayed for him, was faithful in ALL, and loved him, that was enough. I mean, I was giving all of the parts of myself I thought I was supposed to give in a marriage. I thought I was checking off all the boxes and that I would never have to be worried if a man would leave me. Even if we argued, I was confident it would smooth over, and we would be right back to normal. Have you ever pondered on the thought that maybe your definition of good does not always equate to their definition of good? Our marriage was under attack, and I never thought a man leaving me could possibly happen, but it did. He left me, and it drove me straight to God.

We were both in a place of unhappiness. Many people won't ever admit it, and they just carry the day along as if things will just fix themselves. People say the first few years of marriage are the hardest. Some people are not easy to love, some people don't love on your level of love, and some people don't know how to accept your way of love. I came from a home where I never saw my parents argue, and they were married for over 50 years, and no matter what my father did or if my mother let that "Little Nassau" come out, they stayed together. I had no clue marriage would be such a challenge. All I could imagine for myself was I would be "THE WIFE," walking around the house in lingerie and cooking in heels, ready for him to get off from work. You see, I told myself that if I ever got married, it would not end in divorce. I was always afraid to let my walls down for someone out of fear of being hurt. I never believed marriage problems could not be fixed if both people worked at it. I just didn't want to ever get to that point. I didn't believe in separation because there is nowhere in the Bible where God granted Separation. Don't confuse my words here; there are people who are not fit for one another, there are people who marry, and even at the altar, they know they are not meant to be together. There are people who don't even marry for love but for convenience and financial stability. I married for life, and I just kept saying this was not happening; I wanted it to be a dream, honestly. I took my vows seriously when I said FOR BETTER OR WORSE. I knew this was my experience of the WORSE.

Marriage is not for the weak. If it were easy, then everyone would do it, and maybe we would see fewer divorces occur. It is not easy to bring together two people from 2 different backgrounds to become one. I walked into my marriage with flaws, as I mentioned before. I could have gone about things a totally different way, but the reality here is it was too late. I was faced with one of the most challenging periods at that moment. Let's be clear, the devil hates marriage, as he hates family and unity. The devil will send people to destroy your marriage, and the enemy will send your closest friends to speak ill of your marriage when theirs is in turmoil. The head of the marriage and the head of the house is the husband, and when the enemy can get the man out of the home, as the Bible states *Isaiah 1:5-6 when the Head is sick, the whole body is sick, the whole heart faint."* The family structure at that moment was dwindling away. To see the person I love walk away is one of the hardest things I would experience, but it is one of the experiences God needed me to go through.

At first, I kept saying, "Is he crazy? Does he know what he has? Plenty of men would be glad to have me." As hurt as I was, I found that my heart still loved him, and even as months went by, I finally found I was able to start praying for him. I was in a place where rejection was God's plan of redirecting my life. God will break you to bless you, and He will do it at times when you least expect it. You may be a woman or young lady, maybe even a teenager who just got a phone call from your boyfriend, and he says, "I no longer want to be in this relationship." You may be reaching out to a man that you have a strong desire for, and he does nothing but block your calls or ignore you. You may have just walked in on your spouse sleeping in bed with another woman, or you may have just come home, and everything on your mate's side of the closet is empty. You may be asking God today, "Why were you rejected and in this place?" God is responding to you, "Be still, I need your attention as I am redirecting you."

Not many women will tell this part of their story. I was embarrassed to be in this place; I could only think about what everyone else would think of me, knowing that a man had left me. It was for my good that he had left. It was an awakening for me to experience healing. I overcame this test! The Bible says we are overcome by our testimony. I overcame this test, which is why I can share my testimony today. There are many women whose spouses have hurt them, walked out on them, abused them, cheated on them, and they are broken, but they pretend they are ok. These women will post on social media with their popular Monday post, MY #MCM (Man Crush Monday), my best friend for life, my boo. Stop lying to yourself. You are camouflaging the hurt, and you need healing from the experience, and you need deliverance, and it can only come at times from this place of stillness with God. Not many will show this side of their hurt for possible embarrassment. I was embarrassed, and no one knew what I was going through. Not even my children in the beginning. I did everything in the beginning to avoid anyone from coming to my home so they didn't see he wasn't there.

During that time, if you had asked me or my spouse how the other was doing, we would simply say "doing good." If you saw us together, we still smiled; he never disrespected me when we were at family gatherings or any outing together. We still managed to make it look good, but it wasn't. I never disrespected him; I honored this man even in his absence, and I never cheated. I learned to keep my distance from him for the reason of not knowing if I could keep my cool. I said God, if I see this man with a woman, I am not sure if that Jeff's blood (my daddy's blood) won't come out. I thought to myself, God, this man bought me a

46

gun and taught me how to shoot it, and I can remember the look on my dad's face when my husband told my dad so proudly that he had just purchased it. My dad gave him a look like Torri. Are you crazy? I had to ask God to please keep my mind and my emotions under control. I can admit when you feel the level of hurt I was in, all kinds of crazy thoughts come to your mind. Like I wanted him to feel the hurt I was feeling. It is an ungodly reaction to want the people that hurt us to suffer. It was only in my Christian walk as I became stronger in God, I began to pray more for him than wish bad on him.

I was always Mrs. Smith, the removal of the ring on his or my left finger didn't change that. I took my ring off and then was drawn to keep wearing it. I said I made a covenant with God first, and if we were not divorced, I would still honor that covenant, so I wore the ring. No matter where we were, if in each other's presence or not, I was still his wife. You might be saying girl, you are better than me because I would have sent him his divorce papers. Sometimes, you have to give up wanting to handle things your way. Don't miss the lesson because if you are not careful, you can mishandle what God wants you to experience if you don't trust the will of God. I asked God what lesson He needed me to learn in all of this. I am sharing because IT TOOK A WOMAN LIKE ME to stand here and say it happened and I didn't lose my mind. I found that my walk with God became stronger. I didn't go crazy; I didn't give up on my marriage, and I didn't forget that weeping may endure for a night, and joy would come another morning. I still lived through the hurt, the tears, and the sadness. Nothing can stop a woman who is determined and has the will to live. I LIVED!! The more I began to do things to better myself, I found myself releasing the sadness. I found my tears were drying up. The more I read my Bible on the days I was discouraged, the more I would speak the word of God over myself. During the times I worried about who he was with or where he was, God began to tell me to rest in Him, and He would not put more on me than I could bear. I am certain if a man is for you, there is nothing that will stop him from being with you, as men know what they want and when they want you. I prayed so that God would intervene in His will, and it would not be my will. The nights I couldn't sleep, God reminded me of Psalm 91, which says, "*He that dwelleth in the secret place of the highest God shall abide under the shadow of the Almighty.*" As months and even years passed, I began to feel what sweet sleep really meant. God will not fail. I didn't lose because my trust is in God.

During this season, God kept me, He kept my mind, He kept my heart, He increased my finances, and improved my life in its entirety. God does not have to double back on anything because He gets it right the very first time around. God knew the plan He had for me. You may be here; you may be a wife wiping her own tears in a place of loneliness, darkness, sadness, and depression; you are hurt because of who walked out on you, who left you. God knows you, my dear, by your name. God knows the pain you face; he sees every one of your tears. Stop crying, stop worrying, stop questioning God, and start believing what you are facing is a place to be redirected. God is changing the outcome for you. God knew I would go through this. God taught me to just sit still in it and rely on Him to manifest what He had to. I know God was present at my wedding when we said our vows on that beautiful day on the beach, and God was still present in this.

God was reminding me that HE needed to be first in my life. This moment was to bring me to Him. God used this very broken moment to rebuild me. God chose me to go through the test, to break me down to a low place, just to show me that He never left me and that He would reorchestrate my life to a beautiful place in Him. You have to understand to be chosen for a purpose, to be chosen and handpicked it will cost. I remember I told God I wanted to be used by Him, and you must recognize the words we speak have power. To be used by God may be the beginning of a spiritual breaking. You say God use me; be ready for the test to come with that request. God will gut us like a fish and clean us up. Not every woman will be able to stand firm and put her faith in God to move when He wants to move.

In this part of my story, I am sharing the vulnerable side of my life. When you discuss this part of my story with another woman, make sure you discuss that I OVERCAME! I want you to get it in your head that people do leave you. Relationships can be beautiful, and at other times, they can get really ugly and need to be rebuilt or completely dissolved. People will walk away from you. Don't ever allow someone's action to cause you to stay in a low place. If they leave you, just make sure they don't find you in the same place where they left you. Ask God what He is revealing to you in the circumstance. You then will become a WOMAN LIKE ME, an overcomer. You might be holding your story, so I challenge you to release it. You just may be the story of someone's breakthrough. I found myself in this pain, reaching harder for God. I found it was the will of God that I would work on myself alone. I would rebuild my relationship with God rather than just a relationship with a man. I believe that when God wants something from you, He will get your attention one way or another. God got my attention and has kept it ever since. I thought I could fix it the way I wanted to; I thought I would make everything better. I couldn't, and when I told you, God taught me what patience looks like and what stillness really means. God always knows what and who is best for our life. God can bring you from the Pit to the Palace like he did Jacob. One thing I am certain of, as the Bible states in *Hebrews 13:4*, *"Marriage is honorable in all, and the bed undefiled: but whoremongers and adulterers God will judge."* Right after that, in *Hebrews 13:5, it says, ".I will never leave you or forsake you."* I found a place of peace in my stillness; I found God in my alone time.

A moment of stillness requires you to have patience. The Bible reminds us of an important instruction and command in *Psalm 37:7: "Rest in the Lord and wait patiently for Him.* Have you ever been in a season where you wanted to hear from God? Have you ever needed direction on where to go? I can recall praying more than ever to God because I was uncertain about this period in my life, and it was driving me insane. I have many examples of praying and saying, "God, please give me direction." I was in a moment when I wanted to make a decision, and I wasn't quite sure what route to take. I am glad I wasn't hasty in my decision and took a moment to be still and hear from God. The outcome with God will always be far greater than what anyone could imagine. I began to understand the reward from heaven came from me doing absolutely nothing and God doing absolutely everything He always promised He would.

The ability to be still in a moment where the environment or world around you is chaos is a skill set that requires the help of God. Most people cannot sit still and just do NOTHING. I am guilty of it, for sure. There was a point when I would use my own judgment, acting out of pure emotion or anger, making decisions with vengeance or payback, moving hastily, and causing more harm than good. Maybe you are at this very place today. Maybe you have been contemplating moving to another state or city and saying to yourself, "I gotta get out of this place." Maybe you are dealing with a medical diagnosis and are required to give your doctor an answer about whether you should have that procedure or surgery. I am certain there is someone asking themselves, "Should I file for divorce? I love them, but I don't know if I should stay." Are you the young lady who is dating someone, and your heart says one thing, but your mind says the total opposite?

Here is a bit of advice to ponder first, moving to another state doesn't always resolve your problems. The answer to a marital problem is not always divorce, especially if you need healing from past hurt or trauma, or maybe you need to disconnect from a soul tie. Medical concerns can sometimes be resolved with a change in habit and lifestyle without surgery. Sometimes, you're dating or in a relationship when you really should be single and learning to love yourself. Having said all of that, I believe if these are things you are experiencing, this is the time you need to BE STILL so you can receive clear directions. Directions that are biblical and straight from God. *Mark 4:39* teaches us the story of how Jesus spoke to the storm and said unto the sea," Peace, BE STILL." It is in the very same verse that the wind ceased, and there was a great calm because Jesus knew of the storm before the boat left shore. Jesus was so powerful that it only required Him to speak to cause everything to cease.

Don't you know that God can speak to your circumstances, and you must obey the voice of God? I don't care what it is or who you are. When God speaks, even the sea has to obey, every creature has to obey, and every demon has to cease. Stillness requires you to show control in the midst of chaos. You must learn to trust God to silence the storm in your life. He is not threatened or moved by how great the storm is. God is saying to you, today, "BE STILL and stand steady in your Storm."

There is a period in your life when God causes situations to occur just so He can get your attention, and He will get the Glory out of the outcome. There are events that will take place, and the only way you will be set on the right path is if you sit still. We cannot hear from God when we are busybodies. Sometimes you have to sit home and skip Sunday Brunch or Saturday night dining with the girls, and for a good reason.? After you dress up, get cute, and take pictures, you will come back home still broken and in a mess. Who are you fooling? You are following directions from friends and family when, instead, you need to be in a place where God can speak to you. Let's face it, most of the people you may be hanging around and discussing your business with have worse situations than you. Listen to me when I tell you that time alone with God will put you in a place and posture to hear clearly. You will know then that your stillness was worth the brief moment of being uncomfortable.

I can only tell you this from experience. I spent time alone, probably longer than the average person could tolerate. Yes, of course, I was tired of waiting. I was tired of what I thought my life should have manifested at my age. I had no choice but to pray. I prayed for the strength to keep going in spite of what I felt, to build myself up with happiness, and to find peace in silence. I prayed to be ready to move on with my life. Ready to get back on the dating scene because I wanted the companionship, the couples' night, the holding hands; I wanted protection back in the home, the touching. I had to quiet my thoughts and not allow the feeling of loneliness to run me to a sinful place. I was ready to move into what I thought my life should be like. I know if I had, I would not be able to allow this purpose to manifest. I remember my Spiritual Mother, Pastor Zellia, would tell me, "Daughter, don't you move." You see, stillness is not easy because we have the habit of wanting to do something when we don't SEE anything changing in our circumstances.

It pays a lot to walk with God. I had no other choice but to remain in a position to get to a place of wholeness, and I know it will take A WOMAN LIKE YOU to commit to the same act. Many women would walk away when faced with this level of pain. IT TOOK A WOMAN LIKE ME to keep my head high, never quit, be a faithful wife in all, keep dressing and showing up, and let God handle the fight. I smile because I have found happiness and peace in God. I became a better version of myself. I got wiser; my career began to align as I was promoted twice; I ventured out and created another stream of income, took trips, and took myself to the upscale restaurant. I worked hard in my Real Estate business, but most importantly, my spiritual walk was elevated. My praise changed. My prayer life became personal, and God filled the empty space. I could see my spouse, and I had no hatred or regret for him. I became a woman who fought the battle on my knees. I won the victory in my stillness with Jesus on my side, despite it all; I didn't lose myself in the pain. IT TOOK A WOMAN LIKE ME to shift my stillness to my place of elevation in God.

CHAPTER 5

Mannn Girl, Your Emotions

I was the type of woman who, in a heated argument, was going to make you hear me. I never thought I was an argumentative person until I found out that when I became extremely angry, it was hard for me to keep calm and control my emotions. I was never a physical fighter, but I was never afraid to defend myself or the people I loved without thinking twice. I could use my words if I felt you were lying, cheating, being rude, or disrespecting me in any form. I was kind, caring, and thoughtful, and some people think if you are kind-hearted or carry these characteristics, you are a pushover. Not so with me because I could go toe to toe with you with my tongue when needed. I used to tell people I was not going to tongue-tassel with you for the sake of knowing that I didn't have a limit when I got started.

I married a silent tornado, to say the least; if our conversation was getting a little hot, he would get quiet, and if he wasn't ready to respond, he wouldn't. A totally different level of emotional control I didn't have. I, on the other hand, needed to speak my peace (which really wasn't peace at all) and would not stop. I have had times when I was engaged in a conversation with someone and would sit and hold my mouth just for a moment. I was waiting for the right time to interject because when that button got pushed, I was gonna give you a few words. I would respond without really hearing anything the other person in the conversation said because rather than listening to the whole matter, I was listening to respond.

I had to learn how to control my mouth- with the help of God, of course. I had to learn to allow people to speak and not always respond at that moment. It was tough at first because we have a tendency to just respond with the first thought that comes to mind or act without processing the situation in its entirety. All of these reactions are rooted in being an emotional responder. The Google dictionary defines emotions as "*a natural instinctive state of mind deriving from one's circumstances, mood, or relationship with others.* All I can say is if you are a reflection of me, "MANNN GIRL, YOUR EMOTIONS."

My sisters, in recent years, laugh when we get together and will tell people "Kami says what she needs to say, but she doesn't have to yell to cut you or get her point across." I laugh when they mention this because it wasn't always that easy for me to control myself. I was a quiet storm, and I would get you back and feel real good about it. A lot of times, after I said what I said and felt like I was finished, then the conversation was over. Is that you? Do you find yourself not knowing how to handle your emotions? Do you find yourself reacting and putting yourself in a place of danger and regretting your words or actions after the fact?

We can be emotionally driven in our decision-making. Being emotionally driven caused me to not think with a clear mind, just making what I call cloudy decisions. If you are responding to anything in emotion, I can guarantee that was not a good decision you just made. If you respond to a situation with a cloudy mind, you are not thinking clearly. You cannot see the big picture, and the need to just be right is what you communicate. The act of giving up the need to be right is an act that comes with sacrifice and humility. I learned that from my children, believe it or not. They would say I was lecturing them but didn't hear them. I had to really humble myself; you know, even your own children can teach you things about yourself that you really don't see? They were educating me on my own errors or a place that I needed to improve.

We all are flawed in some areas, and you cannot always see the real you, but there will come a time when the people closest to you reveal that person you didn't know really existed. I had to accept that even in their eyes, I was just being emotional. They always said I was very emotional, and yes, they were correct because I began to notice I portrayed extreme sensitivity and would cry when I was angry. I started to recognize those habits formed in my younger years as a child. I would love so hard; I mean, I love hard, but it angered me, and my siblings said my eyes would turn fire-red. You would have to get out of my way because I was kind, but I did not play either. Anger is an emotion that the Bible says in *Ecclesiastes 7:9, "Be not hasty in the spirit to be angry: for anger resteth in the bosom of fools."* Yes, it is ok to be angry, but what is the response and reaction you give during the state of that emotion? Are you a fool? I was, on occasion, acting out just as the Bible instructed me not to, with a hasty reaction. Thank God today for deliverance. Thank God that I learned to be cautious with words, careful in how I made others feel, respectful, and think of what would be the reaction that was Godly and not that of an emotional and uncontrollable response.

Have you ever been in a place where your reactions and response to a situation did major damage to the other person? Have you been at a place where you could, as my father would say, "bust someone's head open to the white meat?" I have. I have been in a rage and cried hysterically from uncontrollable emotions. If you are here, you have to take control of how you respond. We are women and men who act first and think later. This is how so many people end up in prison or physically harmed, killed, or abused. They don't think, pray, turn the other cheek, sit still, and do nothing before they react. You have to manage your reactions to things or people that come to disrupt your peace. It is evident that some people will attack you just because they want to take you to another level. Don't give them power or privilege to see you fail yourself.

You control the narrative, and no one else does. It has been evident to me that living a walk with God brings about peace and a calming spirit. I am at a place where I don't let anything or anyone shift me from the peaceful state I am in. There is a saying, "If it costs me my peace, it's too expensive." Nothing shall disturb you or move you out of your place with God. It is spiritual maturity to achieve this level of control over your response. Take time to think of what could go wrong if you react quickly. Think of who else is affected in the manner you carry yourself and how you speak. Are you cutting people with your words? Are you causing others to not care for your company because they never know how you will react? Do you feel regretful for not handling your situations with silence?

The Bible states in John 14:27, *"Peace I leave with you, my peace I give unto you: not as the world giveth, give I unto you."* There are some things and people that you have to give vengeance to God. I am not wishing pain or harm on anyone; I am speaking scripture. Lead from a heart of love, and do everything to live at peace with your sisters and brothers. Pause and process in every conversation, every reaction, every chance you get. Ask God to guide your tongue, your heart, and your emotions. You will find that your life will become peaceful, and you will no longer be disturbed by anyone or anything. Remember to leave everything to God and MAN YOUR EMOTIONS.

CHAPTER 6

It Takes Faith & Fight

If you ever get the chance to study Hebrews Chapter 11 in the Bible, you would be entering into what some people call the Chapter of Faith. The very first scripture states, "Now faith is the substance of things hoped for, the evidence of things not seen. The Bible shows us in this chapter the Heroes of Faith. The examples show us that though they all were tested, they fought and kept trusting in God and had the faith to believe that God would not fail them. Can you have the faith to believe during the times when the evidence is not seen, when the trial or test you face seems completely hopeless? There is a season that we enter in our lives that will require FAITH and FIGHT.

There is a struggle to have faith and fight for something you cannot see with the physical eye. Are you fighting for something that seems like a hopeless cause? Are you fighting for your children, who seem to be a product of the streets and not a product of the teachings and beliefs that you instilled in them from their youth? Are you fighting for your marriage when your spouse seems to have already gone on with their life without you, and the only thing holding you together is just a name? Are you fighting for your family member who has decided they desire to be affiliated with the LGBTQ community? Are you fighting for a sick parent or child who the doctors have given up on? Are you single and fighting against fornication because all you desire is the touch of a man? Are you fighting demons and witchcraft because you decided to listen to your friend and get counsel from a witch when you knew it was against every Biblical principle you ever knew? Are you fighting the adulterous spirit because you know the Bible says a whoremonger and adulterer God will judge? (yes, leave that woman's husband or that man's wife alone) Are you fighting an addiction? If this is you, you better get up and have faith and fight to get through these phases. You will need the faith that can move these mountains out of your life. You are seeing the mountain, but you need faith to believe that God can and will remove the mountain from the way. Not only will you need to have faith, but the word of God says in Matthew 17:21 that this kind of goeth is not out but by PRAYER and FASTING. So take heed and prepare a time of fasting and prayer. Fast and pray, and be very obedient and persistent in this season. Fasting and prayer might just be the only thing that will get you to the level of faith you need to succeed.

The woman I have become recognized that I had power within. That power only came to fruition when I stepped back and saw that I was a prayer warrior, anointed, and made stronger by reading the word of God and armed for different spiritual battles. God gave me the armor to fight and win the battle on a spiritual level. You see, what you think is natural is really spiritual. You're praying against the man, woman, child, or circumstance when you should pray that the anointing and Spirit of God intervene. Pray and cast down the wickedness by pleading the blood of Jesus over your family, over the sickness, over the marriage, etc. For we wrestle not against flesh and blood but against principalities, against powers, against the rulers of the darkness of this world, against spiritual wickedness in high places Ephesians 6:12. This is why the Bible is written to show you the examples of the times where man could not perform the miracle without faith first being activated. It is FAITH and FIGHT that wins the battle!

Do you know the power you really possess? God can and will equip you to fight the battle. I'm not talking about getting prepared for a physical altercation. There are tools that the Bible speaks of that help you to fight. In Ephesians

6:10 "Finally, my brethren be strong in the Lord and in the power of His might. Put on the whole armor of God that ye may be able to stand. How can you go to war with the enemy when you have no armor? You will set yourself up for a losing battle if you are not prepared. You need the armor and sword, which is the Word of God; you need the helmet of Salvation and a breastplate of righteousness. Do you remember the story of David and Goliath in I Samuel 17? David fought the giant Goliath; he was prepared and armed with a Sling and 5 smooth stones. David walked on the battlefield with armor; he used a sling and landed the stone into the center of Goliath's head and killed him. It was not just the stones that won David the battle, but the pure faith that he exemplified before the fight began. God has given you the ability to fight the giants you face in your life, and with God, you, too, will be victorious. You have to have the faith to believe that you see the giants falling. Take the word of God, dust off that Bible that has been sitting on your nightstand like it is just decoration or accessory to your bedroom. Take the Bible and open it up, begin to read it, and begin to speak the words that you see. The Bible is the way of life; it is the Sword that will slay any circumstance to pieces. The enemy cannot defeat a woman or man who is equipped.

Faith requires that you fight to SEE it before you actually SEE it. You have to begin to talk faith and walk the good fight of faith. Your weekly routine will require you to read and study the word of God; the Bible is a self-help life guide that will assist you in building up your most holy faith. It doesn't just stop with you reading the Bible. You must also attend church because if you are weak, you will need spiritual guidance and a covering to help guide you and teach you. You need a Leader or Spiritual Apostle & Pastor who has faith like Abraham. Who walks and talks faith. Abraham was a man of crazy faith. When Abraham walked up the mountain with his only son Isaac as a sacrifice, he knew that God would intervene. Abraham activated his faith and believed God could not fail no matter what he saw. At the very moment of sacrificing his only son, God provided him with the sacrifice. It is your spiritual leaders in your ministry who should stand in the gap for you when your faith is diminishing. They will help hold you up in prayer because their faith walk is great.

You also need friends and family who can intercede and pray for you during those times you want to just give up. There will be a day that you wake up, and you may not want to move forward; you may find yourself being discouraged because what you see is not proving to improve. You may want to go back to your sinful nature or lifestyle that you have been fighting so hard to be delivered from. You may begin to see that your children are becoming more rebellious, you may see your sick parents' health deteriorating, you may see your spouse completely blocking you out of their life, and you may see your bank account to its last few dollars. You may see NOTHING changing, but there are times when God is silent, and even though you can't see it, you have to believe that GOD is working it out for your good. Don't give up; keep the FAITH and KEEP FIGHTING. YOU ARE THE WOMAN who will not run but face every battle with FAITH. It took a woman like me to stand in faith and fight. I didn't see my life changing when I was faced with pain, but I kept fighting, I kept believing, and I kept the faith. God is not a man that He should lie, and if He said it, it will come to pass.

CHAPTER 7

Restoration

*A*fter you have suffered a while, God will restore you, make you perfect, establish, strengthen, and settle you, I Peter 5:10. This scripture is another one of my favorites, as it was the epitome of what God did for me personally. During one of my hardest seasons, I noticed hours were turning into days, days were turning into weeks, and weeks turning into months, and then, before I knew it, I was down 2 years and not seeing a change in my circumstances. As time progressed, I really was fighting against my own thoughts of believing that God had to be upset with me concerning some past event in my life. I begin to think, ok, this may be my payback for a sin I committed years prior. I was wondering if God really loved me like the Bible says in *Jeremiah 31:3: "I Have loved you with an everlasting love."* God could not dare love me and put me through hell, no, not me. In the place I was in, I felt like God was no longer concerned with the pain I felt in my heart.

Have you ever thought that about yourself? Have you ever started replaying all the nasty things you did to someone going as far back as when you were 10 years old lol? I kid you not. I was really beating myself up trying to just get an understanding with God on His reasoning for this pain. Being stubborn, never trying to reason with God, and questioning His actions didn't work. Then I remembered the story of Job. Job was a righteous, God-fearing man. The Bible states in *Job 1:1 that Job was a perfect and upright man and one who feared God and eschewed evil.* Job 1:7 states how the devil was going to and fro on the earth, and God asked satan *1:8, "Hast thou considered my servant Job?"* If you just read it correctly, God offered Job to be tested by satan. God offered him for the test! All of his possessions were taken, Job became stricken with sores and sick, lost his wife, and all his children died. Tested in every possible way, from his family to his riches. Read the story for yourself to understand that with so many losses, God ended up giving Job a double portion. Can you imagine going through and losing all you have and then in an instant when God sees fit to give you back everything plus double the portion of blessings? Job received an increase from God, replenished with more than what he lost. He experienced pure RESTORATION. The loss you are facing today is not a loss; God's ways are not like our ways, nor are His thoughts like our thoughts. If God tested Job, what makes you think you are exempt. Rest assured, if God is taking you through it, He promised that He would never put more on you than you can bear. I started to understand that God had built me for the test and made my shoulders strong enough to carry the weight. IT TOOK A WOMAN LIKE ME to be ripped off so many things to only be restored greater than what I thought was a loss. God is just that kind of God to show you that you are worrying, crying, and fearful because you see with the natural eye. God then, with his loving Grace, can outpour and make you forget the people and things that you lost. You will be a woman like me, finding yourself thanking God that He took you through that season just to show off what He is capable of doing.

The season of restoring is the ability to achieve the recovery of anything lost. As I slept one night, I was awakened by a voice saying, "RESTORATION." I had a time in my life when I would wonder if I was hearing the voice of God or merely listening to my own thoughts. It was very challenging for me to learn the voice of God, especially as a woman who would have a whole movie scene in her head. I mean, I wrote the script, produced the film, and was the actress and the director. I had a very creative mind, and this was not always positive. I knew the voice that I heard on this occasion wasn't me. I was hearing the voice of God. I began to recognize the voice as time progressed. The Bible states, *"My sheep know my voice and a stranger they will not follow."* As I woke up, I began to read my morning scripture, and there it was: *Peter 5:10: "But the God of all grace, who hath called us into his eternal glory, by Christ Jesus after ye have suffered a while, make you perfect, establish, strengthen, settle you. A complete RESTORATION!*

You think God is hurting you. You think God has forgotten you and stopped loving you, but all the while, His plan is to heal you and accelerate you into your position of promise. God is saying to you today, I LOVED YOU SO MUCH, I HAD TO WOUND YOU. But take rest in me; I WILL RESTORE YOU.

CHAPTER 8

In Your Waiting Season Worship

At any given moment, God can take you from waiting on it to walking in it. That place that you have been in, that you have made up in your mind that nothing will ever change; it can change in a split second. What have you done this entire time that you were waiting for your circumstances to finally work in your favor? What were you doing during the time that you have been waiting for the doctor to give you your medical or lab report? What did you do when you and your spouse stopped speaking? No longer building the home you dreamed of, and filed for divorce. What are you doing while your family is in the hospital and the doctor said it's best to place them in hospice? What are you doing at the moment? You have just been terminated from your job, and you have to file for unemployment. What are you doing at the moment? There is an eviction notice on your door, and you have less than 30 days to move. What do you do when you find out that your child has been attempting suicide? What did you do after your family passed and your heart has been heavy? What do you do when you're fighting depression/anxiety and you just can't seem to find the will to live? What do you do when your Ministry doors have to be closed, and you cannot finance the vision you said God gave you? What do you do when your last resort as a business owner is to file bankruptcy and all the money you have invested has no return on your investment? What do you do when the man you married leaves you to raise all the kids alone? What do you do when the members of your church are verbally attacking and lying to you and leaving the ministry? What do you do when you have been waiting to bear a child, and you have spent thousands of dollars to conceive, and each pregnancy is a miscarriage? What do you do when there just seems like no way out of your circumstance? I will tell you what I did. I began to WORSHIP!

The worship experience pushes you into a moment where your mind redirects focus from your situation. Worship will confuse the enemy because the enemy expects you to be captive to the circumstance and feel depleted and defeated. Worship shifts the atmosphere in a blinking of the eye. Think of the infant that is crying, and you begin to bounce them up and down and start laughing and playing with them; the baby changes its cry to a laugh. That is what worship does in the spiritual realm. The most powerful tool God has given you is the power of choice. The power to change your own situation by what you do in the moment. Make a power move and lift yourself from being down and depressed, lift your spirit, and tell the situation you serve a God of power. Why would you allow anything to fool you into believing that you are anything less than the powerful woman God created. I can recall a very good friend once said to me when I was in a place I felt would not change, they said, "Kami, life is not a rehearsal. You don't get these years back." That is something I will never forget. God is saying to you today that it's time to worship me in all things, and I will deliver you. The ability to lift your hands in adoration of the presence of God invokes the Holy Spirit to your rescue.

To everything, there is a season and a time for every purpose under heaven. This is the first scripture in *Ecclesiastes 3, verses 2-8 says, "A time to be born, and a time to die, a time to plant, and a time to pluck up that which is planted; a time to kill and a time to heal, a time to break down, and a time to build up, a time to weep, and a time to laugh, a time to mourn and a time to dance, a time to cast away stones, and a time to gather stones together, a time to embrace, and a time to refrain from embracing, a time to get, and a time to lose, a time to keep, and a time to cast away; a time to rend and a time to sew; a time to keep silence and a time to speak; a time to love, and a time to hate; a time of war and a time of peace."* You may feel defeated because of the place you are in and believe you are too old, underachieved, haven't created the family you dream of, and that it is never going to happen for you. Let me remind you that we serve the AUTHOR of time, and there is no searching for His reasoning why and when.

God does what He does when, where, and how He wants to perform. The Bible states many are the afflictions of the righteous, but the LORD will deliver. Do you know what that means for me and me? We will experience days of defeat; we will be under attack by the enemy; people will walk out and leave us; people will mistreat us and lie to us, and your children may become hard-headed. You will face life and the hardships it brings, such as not getting selected for the job you applied for. You could be at this moment sitting lying on your back in a hospital. Your business may be tanking, and you may be looking for resources to keep the doors open. You could be down to the very last formula of milk for your baby, you could have no money, and your bank account is sitting in the negative, or you could be homeless and sleeping on your friend's couch. So understand you will be afflicted, you will be here. I was here.

The great news about all of these situations is that God promises HE WILL DELIVER.

You are the woman for the job; you are created and selected to break down walls and break generational curses in your family. You are the spouse who will keep their husband in prayer; as the Bible states, "the husband is sanctified through his wife." IT'S GOING TO TAKE A WOMAN LIKE YOU, so get up, woman of God. Wipe your tears, keep pushing, keep striving, don't stop going to church, go to school, pray for your spouse, pray for your children, and show love and kindness with agape love to everyone. Keep WORSHIPING, play that music to put a smile back on your face, and dance in the hallway while you wait for the next door to open for you. Begin at this moment to tell God thank you despite of.

I am a worshiper; I would run to church, especially on the days when I was broken the most. I worshiped God like never before. Whether with tears in my eyes, sadness in my heart, even in the midst of the storm, I worshiped on the days the enemy tried to keep me home in a dark place. I worshiped God, and it became my way out. So take these instructions from the WOMAN LIKE ME, the woman who worshiped until I saw movement from heaven. Lift up your hands and Worship God, close your eyes, and say, "God, I will WORSHIP you in the middle of the mess." I will WORSHIP in the midst of the chaos. I will WORSHIP you when all hell breaks loose. I will WORSHIP you even in pain. I will WORSHIP you when my prayers haven't been answered, and I don't see the results. I will WORSHIP you while I WAIT.

CHAPTER 9

I Told You To Pray

(Dedicated to my father, the late Elder I. Jeff)

Let's be honest: the most difficult but required thing to do when you're hurting is to pray. In the year 2021, my life changed drastically. I don't think I had ever experienced pain in the way I did. I was broken, my life shattered, confused, and angry, and my heart felt as if it had ripped from me in a matter of days. I was at a place where there were days I truthfully felt numb. I was doing everything I could to hold myself in place. I could literally be in your face, smiling and laughing, and deep down inside, I just wanted to break out in a scream. I had no desire to be around anyone; I had spent so many months alone, and I mean alone. This was the year my father became ill and passed, and months later, my spouse left me. It was the most pain I had ever felt. My family was sad to see my father leave us. He was like this perfect point of wisdom when needed. He was comical even when he wasn't trying; he always knew what to say, and he was the man I never questioned if he would ever walk away from his family. He was just there when you needed him. I remember the last day I spoke to my father; it was on his birthday. It was just so crazy because God, all along, was strategic enough to allow the majority of the entire family to have called and spoken to him on this special day. He was celebrating his birthday in the hospital. My brother Isaac (TJ) even tried to sneak him some sweets in the hospital with some change of clothes. I even remember my family planning for him to come out of the hospital. My mom had even brought him a cake. We were certain he would pull through like he had done almost 2 years before. God had other plans.

My father was a praying man, and he had a healing and praying anointing. I can recall the many times I would be suffering from a migraine, could barely speak, and with tears in my eyes, would call his cell phone, and he would answer with his normal "Yes, Jesus loves you, and so do I." As soon as he heard my soft whisper, he knew I was crying, and he would say, "What's wrong, my baby," and I would simply say, "Daddy, please pray for me." I could hang up and drift off to sleep and would wake up, and the pain would be gone. My entire family knew when they were sick, when they needed God, to just call my father. God had performed many miracles and used my father as a conduit.

My father was a real man of God. Let me be clear: when he was in the world and a sinner, he was a sinner, but when he gave his life to Christ, he was on fire for God. I give special recognition to my mother, Janice, the little lady packed with power because, in that season, she never gave up on my father; she prayed and fasted for quite some time. Those prayers eventually came to pass. God changed him to be a great man, and he used to witness the goodness of God. He told many, many stories to so many people about the life he had on the street and how God changed him. He was a living example of how God can clean a man up and place him to work for the good of God. I don't care if we were out of town on vacation; even for the holiday, you were going to hear about God. My father desired for his family and those he knew to be saved and live for Christ. He would tell his grandson, "Don't do no dumb stuff," or he would say, "Get saved, my baby."

My father never wanted to miss a church service or be late; he didn't play with God. I even remember seeing him study and read the Bible for hours. You best believe we had a family prayer in the house; he would anoint you, and the oil would just run down your forehead into your eyes, Lol. He was long-winded, too, so you might as well get ready to be standing for a while when he prayed. I just believed my father had a one-way line straight to heaven. The Bible says the prayers of the righteous man availeth much, and I knew he was a righteous man of God.

There were many people my father prayed for, and before he passed, our family had started a family prayer on Sunday evenings. Little did I know that God had chosen me to receive the anointing of my father. I did not want it! His anointing carried a hefty price and a cost I was not open to receive. The anointing cost me, and the anointing will cost you. It will cost your friends and family, your marriage will be tested, you will be alone, and you will be a target for the enemy. Your life will be a test when you are chosen and anointed by God.

Just pause to think of all the people in the Bible who walked with God. The Disciples who walked with Jesus. They were tormented in death; one was hung upside down, and John the Baptist, a follower of Jesus, was beheaded. It is a cost you pay to walk with God. But it is ever so rewarding when the day He returns and we hear Him say, "Well done!" I remember one day, my father wasn't feeling the best, and he said, "Kami, PRAY." I was like, no, not today. I'm good. My mother said, "Your daddy said, I TOLD YOU TO PRAY!" You see, at the time, I was really going through a lot in my own life, and I didn't feel like disclosing my business to my family, but praying was just not what I wanted to do at the time. I was the one that needed prayer more than anything. I felt like I was thrown a ball, and God would not allow me to throw it back or release it to someone else. I tried to ask them about letting one of my other siblings pray, but they said no. The Bible says obedience is better than sacrifice. Though I didn't want to pray, I was obedient to my father, my natural and, most importantly, my spiritual Father.

It was only a few months after he told me to pray that my father passed. I had begun to lead the family prayer and build up my own faith by doing so. I didn't know it at the time, but God was preparing me for what he had hand-picked me to do. We never truthfully see where God is taking us when we are hurting. We only recognize in hindsight what the pure orchestration and hand of God over our lives was. The passing of my father was also the birthing of a spiritual gift in me. Through my pain, God was preparing me for a higher calling in Him. I sometimes think that my father knew I had to, and I also believe he never told me because he knew what came with it. He would always say, "Kami, you have a gift from God," I only thought it was because I was a dreamer as a child. I would dream, and my dreams would be warnings of what would come to pass.

Praying is the action that is required to communicate and connect one-on-one with God. His ears are open to the righteous, and the Bible states in *Isaiah 65:24, "And it shall come to pass that before they call, I will answer, and while they are yet speaking, I will hear."* My prayer life became so elevated that there were some days I would get a call to pray for someone, and little did I know God would use me to pray, and He would answer in healing and breakthrough. I went to God for everything; even when I was hurting, I still prayed, and even when the prayers didn't get an immediate answer, I prayed some more. I prayed, I worshiped, and I spent time with God. In the morning, I prayed and talked to God; on my way to work, I prayed and talked to God; when I came home, I prayed; before I went to bed, I prayed. I realized God was beginning to answer my prayers just in the moment I needed Him most. I prayed for so many people, people that I would never expect. I remember even praying with one of my sister's closest friends the day before she passed. I was so hesitant to pray at this time, but I had no choice but to be obedient. Sometimes, my phone would ring, and I could feel there was an assignment coming from God that I had to adhere to. I recall asking God for something for myself and praying, and He wasn't answering me; I then understood that God really needed me in this season to focus only on Him and fulfilling my own personal desires. I don't know if you've ever been here, but if you have, I order you to be obedient to God.

There is evidence that prayer works. I am evidence that prayer works. Your blessings today could be the prayers your mother, father, or grandmother/grandfather prayed for. If you have someone in your life today who prays for you, be sure to keep them in your prayers. The devil attacks them on a whole different level. If there is someone who is sending up a prayer for you, if your spouse prays for you, if your parents pray for you, if you have a Pastor who prays for you if there is a special someone who prays for you, they are fighting for you in the spiritual realm. That, my dear, is a person who loves you dearly. They love you to the point that they are covering and protecting you without you knowing.

Think back over your life for just a moment, and I can guarantee there is something that you prayed about years ago. You are living in that answered prayer. My life was on the verge of going back into a life of sin. I can be honest because I want to be sure I help someone that needs it. I was tempted in my pain to just go back to a sinful lifestyle, do what I wanted to do, and go where I wanted to go. I was starting to believe at one point that what is the purpose of me doing good if I am going to be hurt in the process? My prayer life is what saved me. My prayer life is what snatched me out of the enemy's hand. God anchored me through my prayer life and kept me grounded.

I was also the daughter who had enough strength to pack up my father's belongings at the house after a while of him being gone. As I packed up his area by his bed, there was a page ripped out of the Bible and just left where he slept, and it was highlighted in *John 10:10*, which reads, *"The thief cometh not, but for to steal, and to kill, and to destroy: but have come that they might have life and that they might have it more abundantly."* Next to it, my father wrote, "DON'T LET THE ENEMY CURVE YOU!" I knew it was God that used my father. I would not take anything back that has happened in my life. I don't regret not one second of pain. I don't regret the rejection or the intentional hurt from others. God had a purpose and a plan. I am glad that I was chosen to PRAY! I am glad that I accepted the anointing that God gave me. I am glad that through my father, I understood that when God requires you to do something, there is no pain that should prevent you from being obedient. My father was sick, and for many days, his body was in so much pain, but he still prayed; he still called on God for his family. He prayed for your healing when he was in need of a touch from God. He taught me the importance of praying through the process. It TOOK A WOMAN LIKE ME to pray. I PRAYED even for you.

CHAPTER 10

I Was With God

You never have to make a point to the world or announce where you are in God. The residue will show without your public announcement. You will not have to post on your social media every blessing God has done for you or the elevation that God has taken you. You won't have to discuss that you have changed and are not the same person because everyone will have front-row seats to witness that you were with God. There is a light that will shine from you that will speak without words. If you set aside everything you had pre-planned for your life and allow God to have His will manifest, you will become a new being. The life that showcases will be what inspires and encourages. You will have a spiritual attraction that people will begin to gravitate to.

Life is fragile, life is a gift, life is thriving, and every day is worth living it. Once I made God my priority, my life began to align. God put me in a place where I could only depend on Him. God put me in a place of preservation. Like fine wine in a new wineskin, you too can become a representation of a new being as we die to our old selves and ways. I want you to understand that time heals wounds, as some will say, but preservation will advance you. You may have to go through such a tough time alone. You will wonder if you can keep going and if it is really worth it. It will be the preservation of anything to make it free from damage or decay, the process of keeping the value alive. God is taking you through spiritual preservation.

You must accept that there will be a season that you will be the student and God will be your teacher. Sometimes, that teacher is silent, but it doesn't mean He is not busy working on your behalf. You will be the only person in the classroom, and you will be required to pass the test. Your test will be the testimony for the next woman who will walk the same road or similar test you finally passed. Your alone time with God will be required; you may begin to notice that you are not in the in-crowd, you are not going to the same places, you will desire to please God rather than man, and you will find yourself getting busy working in the vineyard.

It is my prayer that your light shines so that women and men will see your life and understand that God is real. May the anointing and blessings begin to overtake you. May the life you chose be the life that your spouse, children, relatives, friends, colleagues, and business partners begin to recognize that God is all-powerful, knowing, and real. As my life began to anchor in God, people started to see a change in me. I saw a different reflection of myself when I looked in the mirror. I was no longer the same. After reading this book, you must set the stage for a permanent shift. Some people are not going to find you where they left you.

When you understand that God always has a plan and the ultimate goal is for you to inherit the kingdom, you will walk and speak and carry yourself as a royal being. You do remember the word of God says in *Matthew 6:33 to "seek you first the kingdom of God and His righteousness and ALL these things shall be added unto you."* Did you read that sentence in its entirety? ALL, not some, but ALL these things will be added and given to you. Take the limits off of God. Let God amaze you with His power. Let God bless you with His promises.

We serve a God of the impossible. I finally started to get hold of the promises of God. I even tested God. I told Him, "ok, God, let me see what the blessings that maketh rich and addeth no sorrow to it is all about." I tested God on numerous occasions and said, "God, you said you will bless my later days," so I reminded Him of His word. He performed what He said. The Bible says your latter days will be greater than your former days. So every day from this day forth, once you have given God your heart, He can allow you to walk and witness the Latter-day promises. As my Bishop Williams of Holy Tabernacle U.C.O.G. Fl would say, "There is a blessing with your name on it!"

I believed in God, and He showed up. He began to outpour me with favor, favor on my job, favor in my finances, favor in my family, favor in my business, favor in my spiritual walk, favor with healing and breakthroughs. There were moments when I was in shock at what God was doing for me. No, I can't say every prayer I prayed has been answered. There are still prayers I'm waiting on today. I am just patient enough now and crazy enough to believe that it is not a matter of if He can; it is just a matter of if it's HIS WILL.

Start seeing everything from this point forward through a spiritual lens. Start believing that you are greater and more powerful. What you are going through is not driving you crazy. It is DRIVING YOU TO GOD. God needs you, and He is ready for you to break the mold. Get up and build, get up and anoint your home, cover your spouse, cover your children, start that business, and speak over your life and your circumstances. Get up and speak with the authority that God has given you. Tell the devil he is a liar, and today he is defeated. You are the WOMAN God has been waiting for.

You, like me, are the woman who is going to make hell nervous! Go out and step on the neck of the enemy and show him that it will ONLY TAKE A WOMAN LIKE YOU to walk in the power you so greatly possess. This is your season! I WAS WITH GOD, and I am in my season. I walk with my head high, I walk in the anointing of my Father, I speak with authority and believe that there is no weapon formed against us that shall ever prosper, and every word that has been spoken against me on the day of judgment God will condemn. I am a faith walker; I am the lender and never the borrower; I am a worshiper and a leader. I am the CEO; the woman who decrees and declares everything connected to me wins. I am the best to ever do it! I am the woman who did not give in, nor did I ever lose. Do you think what I went through for the years, I did to sit still and be quiet? No, I came to be an example of the freedom and liberty of knowing Jesus. I have never been average, never been a carbon copy of a cheap original. I came to work for God and put my life on display so you will know that there will come a time that you will fight like your life depended on it, and you will pick up the word of God and armor yourself and realize there is no stopping you. I know it TOOK A WOMAN LIKE ME to write this book to show you that it can and will be done.

IT IS WELL.

Made in United States
Orlando, FL
27 July 2024

49616281R00055